Daydreaming with Dad
by Anderson Atlas

Copyright 2018 Anderson Atlas
All rights reserved including the right of reproductions in whole or in part in any form.

Name: Atlas, Anderson
Title: Daydreaming With Dad
Description: Trade paperback edition 1: Synesthesia Books, 2018
Identifiers:
ISBN-10: 0-9974788-9-6
ISBN-13: 978-0-9974788-9-1 (Synesthesia Books)
BISAC Category:
Juvenile Nonfiction: family, fathers, parenting, bedtime, dreams
Subjects:
Father and daughter, father and sons talk, learn and daydream together. Wholesale Available from IngramSparks

To my daughter Ellie. Somethings I had no idea I did not know, until I met you. Thank you for daydreaming with me.

Daddy, how big is Earth?

Big.

How Big?

If we ran across Earth, it will take us about two years.

Geez, I can run across the playground in ten seconds so the world must be pretty big.

And most of it is water, so you'd have to swim a lot, too.

I'm a good swimmer.

I know you are.

Did you know that up isn't really up?

What do you mean, daddy?

Earth is round. So up is really out.

I'm confused.

We're standing on a big ball in space so when we look up, we're actually looking out. The clouds float over the Earth and the rain falls toward the center.

So up is out toward the stars?

Yeah, I think you get it.

Daddy, how do fish breathe under water?

That one's easy. There's air in water.

Like bubbles?

Yeah. But most of the air fish breathe is too small for us to see with our eyes.

Their gills pull the very small bits of air out of the water.

I wish I could breathe underwater.

Me too.

Did you know that humans have walked on the moon?

Really? But the moon is so small.

It only looks small 'cause it's far away.

Have you been to the moon, Daddy?

No, but I would love to go. I'd bring my guitar and play a solo for Earth.

I would dance to your moon song on the moon. That would be fun.

How do you know so much, Daddy?

You get smarter the older you get.

I want to be as smart as you and mommy.

You will. But you might be even smarter.

How?

Read every day, that's how.

I love to read, books are my super favorite.

But Daddy, there are some things I know
that you don't know.
   Really, like what?

I know that my baby sister doesn't eat her broccoli, but hides it in her pocket.

Oh, really?

Yup, she tried to feed it to the puppy, but he didn't like it either.

That's two things I didn't know.

I know that eating too much candy doesn't really hurt your belly like Momma says.

Are you sure about that one?

Oh yeah, I'm sure.

I know that when you snore you sound like a goose with a cold.

Is that so?

Yup, and it wakes me and Mommy up.

You've taught me something, little one.
What's that, Daddy?
It's my favorite thing of all.
What? What did I teach you??
That hugs make everything better.
I think we learned that together.
We are so smart.

Help an indie author out!

Leave a review on Amazon, Goodreads, or your blog. One review takes you minutes, helps an author out for years!

Even if you didn't buy on Amazon, you can still leave a review.

~ thank you so much, ANDERSONATLAS

Read other works published by Anderson Atlas go to:

AndersonAtlas.com

Middle Grade Readers and Young Adult

Contact the Author / Illustrator:
Anderson Atlas
thelostspells@gmail.com
AndersonAtlas.com

Order Copies of this title and others from Synethesiabooks.com

Copies are also available at Amazon.com

www.ingramcontent.com/pod-product-compliance
Lightning Source LLC
Chambersburg PA
CBHW041408160426
42811CB00103B/1547